Note to Parents

Backyard Cruises is designed to help young children fill those long vacation days at home. Projects and ideas for summer and winter fun will trigger their imaginations and provide an outlet for their abundant energy.

Uncle Scrooge's enterprising and penny-pinching antics introduce children to each activity. Of course, the activities are cost-free—Uncle Scrooge would have it no other way. In fact, a few activities may help children earn a little money.

Most of the materials used in this book can be found in and around the house. Cardboard boxes, paper bags, and construction paper are the most needed supplies.

With a few exceptions, the activities will work in any weather suitable for outdoor play. Many of them can be used indoors, as well. The Jiminy Cricket symbol appears with any project or activity that requires adult help.

Because backyard cruises are more fun when friends come along, many activities are designed for two or more children. Expect a yard full of wild animals, pilots, or Olympic contenders—and enjoy the fun.

ISBN 0–7166–2907–0
Library of Congress Catalog Card No. 83–51339

Backyard Cruises

Free Vacation Fun

Published by
World Book Encyclopedia, Inc.
a Scott Fetzer company
Chicago

Letters for Uncle Scrooge

Although Uncle Scrooge enjoyed getting mail, he hated bills even more than most people. Uncle Scrooge was the richest duck in the world—but he really hated to spend money! So when Chives, the butler, would carry in the mail on the silver mail tray, Uncle Scrooge almost always flew into a rage and yelled, "Bills! Bills! Bills!"

But this morning's mail was special. There were no bills on the tray, but there were three letters—one each from Uncle Scrooge's nephews, Huey, Dewey, and Louie. They were all away on a great camping trip.

As Uncle Scrooge took the mail from the tray, he said excitedly, "Stay, Chives. Listen to the letters my nephews have written me."

"Certainly, sir," replied Chives.

"I'll read Huey's letter first," said Uncle Scrooge, ripping open the first envelope. The letter said:

Dear Uncle Scrooge,
This camping trip is super fun! I really am enjoying the great outdoors. My favorite activity is hiking along the rugged trails near where we are camped. I'm having a swell time, but I think Dewey and Louie might be a little homesick.
Your favorite nephew,
Huey

"It sounds as if Huey is having a wonderful time, eh, Chives?" inquired Uncle Scrooge.

"Indeed, sir," answered the butler.

"But poor Dewey and Louie," Uncle Scrooge said. "I was afraid that the great outdoors might be too much for them to handle. Let's see what poor, homesick Dewey has to say." Sadly, Uncle Scrooge tore open the second letter and read:

Dear Uncle Scrooge,
Wow! Camping is something special! The weather is just great. I could stay here forever, but I'm not so sure about Huey and Louie. They both act a little homesick.
Your favorite nephew,
Dewey

"Hmm, Chives," said Uncle Scrooge, raising an eyebrow. "It sounds as if Dewey is enjoying himself, too."

"Possibly, sir," smiled Chives.

"Well, poor Louie. Poor, lonely Louie. Let's see how unhappy he sounds in his letter," said Uncle Scrooge. He read:

Dear Uncle Scrooge,
What a neat time I'm having here! Sleeping in a tent is lots of fun. The best part of camping is watching the wild animals all around our camp. I'm having so much fun that I may never come home.
Your favorite nephew,
Louie
P.S. Huey and Dewey are really homesick.

Uncle Scrooge was silent for a moment. Then he said, "Chives, I think each one of my nephews is homesick, but really won't admit it. What should I do? I'd hate to have them give up and come home. Camping really is a lot of fun, and it's good for them to rough it."

"If I might make a suggestion, sir," Chives said, "I believe your nephews would be less homesick if they could talk to you. Perhaps you could put in a phone system."

"Drat!" exclaimed Uncle Scrooge. "That would cost money. These letters might as well be bills!" Then he cleared his throat and said, "Of course, I'll spend money to make Huey, Dewey, and Louie happy."

"Sir," replied Chives, "if you will allow me, I believe I can make a telephone that will cost you almost nothing."

Uncle Scrooge perked up. "Try, Chives. By all means, try," he commanded.

An hour or so later, Chives returned. He was holding a tin can with a string dangling out of the end. "Sir," he said to Uncle Scrooge, "your nephew Huey would like to speak with you. Simply speak his name, rather loudly, into this can."

"Speak into a can?" Uncle Scrooge asked. "How could that possibly work?"

Before Uncle Scrooge could say any more, he heard Huey's voice calling out of the can, "Uncle Scrooge! Uncle Scrooge!"

Uncle Scrooge quickly grabbed the can from Chives and spoke into it. "Huey! Huey! How's your trip?"

"Just ducky!" answered Huey's voice through the can.

After a long, delightful conversation with Huey, Dewey, and Louie, Uncle Scrooge was beaming. "Congratulations, Chives," he said. "Your telephone is a tremendous success!"

"Thank you, sir," Chives said humbly, "but I was fortunate. If your nephews were in a faraway camp, I could not have stretched a string to reach them. Thank goodness they are camping in your backyard!"

A Backyard Telephone

You can make the backyard telephone that Chives made. Here's how to do it.

What you'll need

2 cans	Hammer
String	Small nail
2 paper clips	

1. Make sure both cans are clean. Turn the cans upside down. Use the hammer and nail to punch a small hole in the bottom of each can.

2. Cut a long piece of string. Thread one end through the hole and into a can. Tie the end to a paper clip. Pull the string from the outside until the paper clip is flat on the bottom inside the can.

3. Repeat this with the other end of the string and the paper clip. Your tin-can telephone is ready to use.

4. Have a friend hold one can. Pull the cans far apart so that the string stretches tightly between them. When you want to talk, put your mouth close to your can and talk. When you want to listen, put your ear close to your can and listen.

Jiminy Cricket says, "Ask for help in punching the holes. And make sure the edges of the cans are smooth."

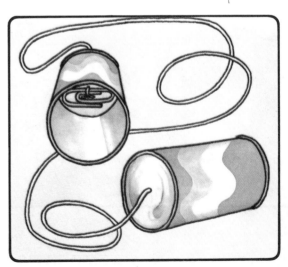

Explorer's Tent

To make a tent like Uncle Scrooge's, pin two old blankets together along one edge. Then have a butler (or another tall person) help you throw the blankets over a clothesline. Spread the blankets apart and put bricks or rocks on the edges to hold them in place.

Picnic Lunch

Your picnic can be an adventure if you add a little extra something to your favorite sandwich. How about honey and apple slices in your peanut-butter sandwich? If you like ham and cheese, add some cucumber slices. Experiment—but think ahead. Only make what you'll really eat!

Fun at Camp McDuck

Although his nephews don't know it, Uncle Scrooge likes to camp in the backyard, too. He makes a homemade tent and packs a picnic lunch in his homemade backpack. Of course, Huey, Dewey, and Louie like backyard camping because it is fun for them to make believe that they are out in a dark forest. Uncle Scrooge likes it because it is cheap.

So, on an early afternoon on a summer day, they might find Uncle Scrooge alone in his backyard with his homemade tent (put up by Chives), his backpack (packed by Chives), and his lunch (served by Chives).

A Homemade Backpack

What you'll need

Large paper grocery bag   Masking tape
Gift-wrap ribbon   Scissors

1. Stick four pieces of masking tape on the side of the bag, as shown. Cut 1-inch (2.5 centimeter) slits through the tape and the bag.

2. Cut two 24-inch (61 cm) pieces of ribbon. Thread each piece through a top and a bottom slit. Tie the ends inside the bag.

3. Cut a 5-inch (12.5 cm) slit down each folded corner of the bag.

4. Fold down the four cut sides of the bag— first the narrow sides, then the front, then the back. Decorate your backpack with paints or crayons. Slip your arms into each ribbon and you are wearing your backpack. (Remember, your backpack is only paper, so don't try to carry heavy things in it.)

Vacation Fun Funds

Uncle Scrooge was proud of Huey, Dewey, and Louie. They were earning money! Just yesterday, they had made a lemonade stand and earned almost two dollars selling lemonade. Today, the boys were going to sell other things.

Late in the afternoon, Huey ran into the house. "Uncle Scrooge!" Huey exclaimed. "I made a stand and sold songs. For five cents, I sang a song. I made fifty cents!"

"Great!" said Uncle Scrooge.

Next, Dewey rushed in. "Uncle Scrooge!" he shouted. "At my stand, I sold violin tunes for a nickel each. I made forty-five cents!"

"That's wonderful!" smiled Uncle Scrooge.

Moments later Louie ran into the house yelling, "I made two dollars and fifty cents at my stand!"

Uncle Scrooge's eyes lit up. "Two dollars and fifty cents!" he shouted. "What did you sell?"

"Ear plugs," said Louie proudly.

You can make a stand, too. First, decide what to sell. It can be lemonade, or something else—a song, a magic trick, a joke, a picture, a poem.

You don't have to sell things for money, either. You could ask for play money, baseball cards, buttons, other magic tricks, or things to trade.

Your stand can be a card table, a big cardboard box, or a wagon. Put it near a busy sidewalk, and decorate it.

Print a big, bright sign, so that people know what you are selling and what it costs. Tape the sign to your stand or a nearby tree, and you're in business!

Here are some ideas to get you started.

Fancy Lemonade Recipe

1 cup lemon juice
4 cups water or soda water
4 tablespoons honey
Put everything in a pitcher and mix well, making sure all the honey dissolves. Add ice and stir.

More Ideas for Lemonade

1. Add red food coloring to make pink lemonade.

2. Add something extra to each glass you serve—a slice of fresh lemon, a piece of fresh mint, or a mint gumdrop.

3. Freeze ice cubes with strawberries or pieces of fruit inside. Add a cube to each glass.

Horsing Around

Uncle Scrooge looked out the window to see Huey, Dewey, and Louie playfully wrestling in the backyard. "Oh my," he thought. "They're just horsing around, but I'd better find something for them to do before they get into a serious fight. Hmmm. Horsing around. That reminds me of a toy I used to make when I was just a little duck. And it was cheap, too."

Just a half hour later, Uncle Scrooge looked out the window again. There were three happy young riders having great fun on their new broomstick horses.

Here's how Uncle Scrooge made broomstick horses.

Jiminy Cricket says, "Ask for help with cutting."

What you'll need

Broomstick	String
2 paper lunch bags	Ribbon
Shredded newspaper	Tape
Construction paper	Scissors

1. Cut two 1-inch (2.5 centimeter) slits at the top corners of one bag. Fold the back flap down. Fill the bag up to the slits with newspaper.

2. Fill the second bag with newspaper and shove it onto one end of the broomstick. Tie the bag closed around the stick. (Use tape to hold the bag in place.)

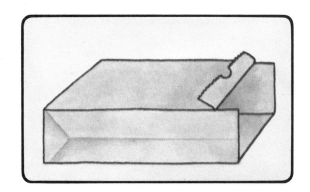

3. With tape, attach the first bag to the top of the second. The folded flap on the second bag should cover part of the front of the first.

4. Add a ribbon harness and construction-paper ears and hair. Paint eyes, nostrils, and a friendly smile.

5. Now that you have made your horse, here are some backyard games you can play.

Pony Express. Use a schoolbag as a mail pouch to carry the mail from town to town.

Pegasus. In Greek legends, Pegasus was a winged horse. Tape some cardboard wings to your horse and have it carry you above the clouds.

Rodeo Rider. Pin a number on your back and turn your broomstick horse into a wild, bucking bronco.

Horse Show. Prance your horse around the ring. Have it perform fancy bows and turns.

Chips Ahoy

Uncle Scrooge went hunting for a pirate treasure hidden by Huey, Dewey, and Louie. The treasure was chocolate chip cookies, Uncle Scrooge's favorite. He was starving, too. He had counted money all day. That always made him hungry!

The first clue was on the kitchen table. It was a rhyming note that said:

A clue to a treasure good to eat
Is hidden on the blue swing seat.

He found a note on the swing seat that sent him to the gate. More notes and rhymes had him dashing to the porch, lawn chair, birdbath, mailbox, and oak tree. At last, in a hollow of the tree, he found the treasure.

Uncle Scrooge slowly reached into the chest for a cookie. But all he found was crumbs and a rhyme:

We hid the treasure and waited and waited.
But then we got hungry and (Sorry!) we ate it!

Organize your own treasure hunt. Decide what the treasure will be. You can use play money or toy jewelry—or even marbles, bottle caps, or game tokens.

Make your own coins. Just cut out circles of cardboard and wrap them in aluminum foil.

Make a treasure chest from a small shoebox. Paint the box or cover it with construction paper or foil.

Put the treasure in your new chest. Include a warning in the chest for those who find it. "Beware! This is the treasure of the toughest pirate on the seven seas!"

Hide the chest. Put clues on notes to help others find the treasure. The clues don't have to be rhymes. Pictures will do.

It's a Bird! It's a Plane!

Uncle Scrooge was nervous. Huey and Dewey and Louie had nothing to do. When that happened, they often came up with ideas that cost him money—trips to the zoo, the movies, or even an amusement park. Uncle Scrooge had to think of something—fast!

Quickly, he grabbed a cardboard carton and set to work. When he finished, he yelled, "Here you are, boys. This will really make time fly!"

Uncle Scrooge made an airplane from the cardboard box. And that was just the beginning of the fun. Huey, Dewey, and Louie made a backyard landing field, using long pieces of string to mark the runway. They made a control tower from a chair and took turns telling when it was safe to land.

Make your own cardboard plane and enjoy your flight. Why not stop at Duckburg and visit Uncle Scrooge?

What you'll need

Large cardboard carton
   with flaps
4 brass fasteners

Nail
Scissors or knife
Rope or heavy string

1. Carefully cut the flaps off the box. They will be the wings.

2. On each side of the box, cut a narrow slit starting 1 inch (2.5 centimeters) from the end. Make it as long as the narrow side of the flap.

3. Cut an opening in the bottom of the box, behind the slits. It should be big enough for you to lift the box up around yourself.

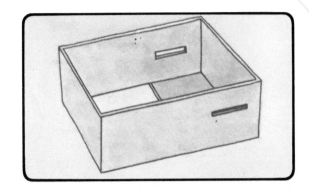

4. Slip the end of a long flap into each slit, leaving about 2 inches inside the box.

5. Lay the short flaps across the ends of the wings inside the box. Hold one flap above and one flap below the wing to make a "sandwich." On one side, punch two holes through all three layers of the sandwich. Push brass fasteners through the holes. Repeat on the other side.

6. Punch two holes near the top of the front and the back of the box. Tie pieces of rope through the holes for straps.

7. Step into the box and put the straps over your shoulders. You're ready for takeoff!

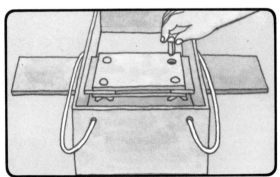

Jiminy Cricket says, "Ask for help when cutting and punching holes."

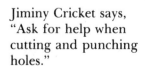

Sidewalks
and Driveways

Uncle Scrooge treasures more than just money. He
treasures his nephews and his friends. He treasures
good new ideas and good old ideas—particularly if they
are cheap. Here are some good old ideas that Uncle
Scrooge thinks you will like.

Hopscotch

There are lots of ways to play hopscotch. These rules are for Pattern 1. You can use the other patterns, too. Draw them with chalk on a sidewalk or driveway.

1. Stand behind the throwing line. Try to throw a stone into square 1.

2. If your stone lands in square 1, hop on one foot over square 1 to square 2. Continue hopping in each numbered square, without touching the lines. When you jump into the double squares (4-5 and 7-8), you put a foot in each square.

3. When you reach square 9, turn around and hop back. At square 2, bend over and pick up the stone in square 1. Then hop into square 1 and out.

4. Throw the stone into square 2. Hop into square 1, square 3, then on to square 9 and back again. Do this for each number, always hopping over your stone. Use the Sky Blue space when you must hop over square 9 to avoid your stone.

5. Your turn ends if you miss a throw, step on a line, or touch both feet to the ground (except on double squares or Sky Blue).

Pattern 1

Pattern 2

Pattern 3

Fortune telling

Use a jump-rope rhyme to tell your fortune. Your first question is, "What will I be when I grow up?" You jump "red hot peppers" (very fast) and say:

Rich man, poor man, beggar man, thief,
Doctor, lawyer, merchant, chief,
Tinker, tailor, cowboy, sailor.

Whatever name you miss on is what you will be—at least, until next time you play.

You can ask other questions, too. Here are some:

Where will I live when I grow up?
(Big house, little house, pigpen, barn.)
What kind of clothes will I wear?
(Silk, satin, cotton, rags.)
What kind of ring will I wear?
(Diamond, ruby, emerald, glass.)

If it's not jump-rope weather, just count down the buttons on whatever you are wearing while you say the names. The name that falls on the last button is the answer to your question.

21

Splash!

It was a hot, sticky day. "I've got to cool off," Uncle Scrooge thought as he drove home. Suddenly, as he passed the Duckburg Car Wash, a great idea came to him.

Later that afternoon, Chives was shocked to see Uncle Scrooge in the backyard, happily splashing in a spray of water from a strange-looking, homemade machine. Even more surprising, Uncle Scrooge's piles of gold were wet and sudsy.

"Sir, what are you doing?" Chives gasped.

"Oh, Chives," Uncle Scrooge replied, "I'm having a delightfully cool *coin* wash."

You don't have to build a big contraption to cool off. You can have fun with some of the things Uncle Scrooge used in his coin wash. You can float, sink, sprinkle, spray, or fill and empty these:

funnels	coffee cans
straws	sponges
measuring cups	clothespins
plastic spray bottles	plastic strainers
corks	plastic pitchers

Jiminy Cricket says, "Ask for help when punching holes."

Sponge fight

Get together with friends. Soak lots of small sponges in buckets of cold water—and throw. Splat! It's a great way to cool off.

Mini-shower

Punch several small holes in the bottom of a clean half-gallon milk carton. Take it outside. Fill it with cold water and quickly hold it over your head. Don't you feel cooler now?

Water slide

Get a big sheet of plastic. (A plastic dropcloth works fine.) Lay it on the ground and spray water all over it. Now sit down and slide on it, feet first. Then try to slide on your stomach, arms first.

Stargazing

Sometimes Uncle Scrooge just likes to lie in the
backyard, gaze at the stars in the sky, and think. Here
are some poems just for stargazing.

Night

The sun descending in the west,
The evening star does shine;
The birds are silent in their nest,
And I must seek for mine.

William Blake

Twinkle, Twinkle, Little Star

Twinkle, twinkle, little star,
How I wonder what you are!
Up above the world so high,
Like a diamond in the sky.

When the blazing sun is gone,
When he nothing shines upon,
Then you show your little light,
Twinkle, twinkle, all the night.

Jane Taylor

Star-Light, Star-Bright

Star-light, star-bright,
First star I see tonight;
I wish I may, I wish I might,
Have the wish I wish tonight.

Mother Goose

Backyard Olympics

One day, when Huey, Dewey, and Louie were cleaning up Uncle Scrooge's attic, Huey found a box full of medals. "Look at this," he shouted. "There must be a dozen medals here. They each say *Duckburg Olympics, Scrooge McDuck, First Place!*"

"What are the Duckburg Olympics?" asked Dewey.

"That's a bunch of races and contests held every few years. The winners get medals," said Huey.

"Wow!" Louie exclaimed. "I didn't think Uncle Scrooge was good at sports."

Huey laughed and said, "He's not. But these medals for first place are made out of gold."

"Oh, I see," said Louie. "No one would ever beat Uncle Scrooge in a race for gold."

Why not have your own backyard Olympics? On the following pages are some races and contests you can use, and directions for making your own Olympic medals.

Olympic Races

For races, you'll need starting and finish lines. You can lay strings in the grass, or mark lines with chalk on a sidewalk or driveway.

Have separate races for younger and older children, so that everyone has a chance to win. You can start with running (forward and backward), hopping, skipping, and crawling races. Then try these:

Sweater relay. Divide the group into two equal teams. Give each team a sweater. The first member of each team puts on the sweater, buttons it, runs to the finish line, unbuttons it, and runs back. The sweater is given to the next team member, who does the same thing. The winning team is the one whose players finish first. Use sweaters with lots of buttons, and make everyone button and unbutton them all!

Apple relay. Divide all the players into two equal teams. Give each team an apple. Each team member takes a turn walking to the finish line and back, while balancing the apple on his or her head. The first team to finish wins.

Other Olympic Games

You can have non-running Olympic games, too. Play some favorite neighborhood games, or try these:

Clothespin Throw. Cut off the top of a milk carton. Put a few rocks or marbles in it to keep it from tipping over. Place the carton on the ground and mark a throwing line in front of it. Each player stands behind the line and tosses five clothespins at the carton. The player who gets the most inside wins.

Balloon throw. Each player stands behind a line and throws the balloon as far as possible. The spot where the balloon lands is marked with a button. The farthest throw wins. A ball or beanbag can be thrown, too, but a balloon throw gives everyone—not just the best throwers—a chance to win.

Straw Hockey. Stand two shoeboxes on their sides at opposite ends of a small table. Tape the boxes to the table, with the open sides facing each other. Two players sit opposite each other, one behind each goal. They join hands on either side to make a hockey rink. Then, using the straws, each player tries to blow a table tennis ball into the opposite goal. Three goals wins!

Olympic Medals

Make your backyard Olympics even more fun by awarding medals to everyone who plays a game.

Cut out construction-paper circles. Decorate each circle with a picture that stands for the whole backyard Olympics or for a single race or game. Then cut a long piece of ribbon for each medal. Tape the ends of the ribbon to the back of the paper circle. You can use a different color ribbon for each kind of medal you make.

Uncle Scrooge's Parade

A visitor to Duckburg saw a parade joyfully marching down Main Street.

"Is today a Duckburg holiday?" she asked a police officer.

"Oh no, ma'am," replied the officer. "Scrooge

Decorations

Decorate bikes and trikes, big wheels, and wagons for your parade. Weave strips of crepe paper into the spokes of bike wheels. Wrap strips around handlebars, too. Tape streamers to the handles. Make flags by folding a piece of paper in half, putting a long thin stick in the fold, and pasting the halves together. Attach the flags to bikes and trikes, or carry them.

Music

Parades are more fun if you have a band, so take along some instruments that are easy to carry. You can ring bells, beat on boxes, bang pot-lid cymbals, and hum through paper-towel tubes.

McDuck, the richest duck in the world, arranged this parade on his own. He's celebrating."

"Celebrating what? His birthday?" asked the visitor.

"No, ma'am," said the officer. "You see, some years ago, he lost a quarter, and today he found it."

Like Uncle Scrooge, you can have a parade for any reason, big or little—winning a game, celebrating someone's birthday, or welcoming a visitor. The important thing is to have fun and get your friends to march with you. Here are some ideas to get you started.

Special costumes

There are lots of ways to dress up for a parade. Uniforms are costumes. Friends who belong to scouting groups or teams can wear their uniforms. Other friends may have a favorite Halloween costume, or a costume from a play. Old clothes, painted faces, and newspaper hats are fun, too.

Special attractions

If your pet is willing, add it to the parade. (Make sure it's in a cage or on a leash.) Most animals don't like wearing costumes, but your pet probably won't mind having a bow tied to its collar.

Click! Click!

Uncle Scrooge took his camera and his nephew Donald on a long walk through Duckburg Woods. Donald watched while Uncle Scrooge crept through the trees, sneaking closer and closer to a wild animal to get just the right picture of a deer, raccoons, and even a skunk.

A week later, Donald said to Uncle Scrooge, "I'd love to see the pictures you took in the woods."

"Oh, I didn't take any pictures," said Uncle Scrooge.

"But I saw you!" Donald told him.

"I just pretend to take pictures," said Uncle Scrooge. "I would never really spend money on film!"

You and your friends can have a wild-animal photo hunt like Uncle Scrooge's. You'll need two things—a camera and wild animals.

Camera

To make a play camera, glue a spool to the front of a small cardboard box. Attach a string to the sides for a strap. Paint the box black and the spool silver or gray. (You can also use an old camera without film, or a toy camera.)

Wild animals

Make a mask from a grocery bag that is large enough to fit over your head. Cut out holes for eyes. You can cut flaps in the top or sides and push them out for ears. Cut out big parts, such as an elephant's trunk, from another bag and tape them on.

Jiminy Cricket says, "Ask for help with cutting if you need it."

You and your friends can take turns being the animals. Of course, all the animals hide. The photographer finds an animal, points the camera at it, and says, "Click!" The last animal to have its picture taken is the next photographer.

A Little Game of Golf

Uncle Scrooge used to lose his temper easily, especially when he played golf. In fact, he had to quit playing, because every time he lost his temper he broke his golf clubs.

With a little help from Chives, Uncle Scrooge set up his own backyard golf course. Now he's a much more relaxed duck. He never loses his temper when he plays golf in his own backyard. Well, almost never.

You can play backyard golf, too. Here's what you'll need.

A ball

You don't need to use a real golf ball. A small rubber ball or a table-tennis ball will do.

A golf club

To make a golf club, find a smooth stick about two feet (60 centimeters) long. Push the end all the way into a small plastic bottle. Wind strong tape around the neck of the bottle and the stick.

Golf course

Make a golf course with several holes. Mark a starting spot, or "tee," for each hole. Several yards (meters) away, make the hole. It can be a circle of string laid on the grass or an open paper lunch bag laid on its side. A few stones inside the bag will hold it in place.

You can make your course tricky by building little hills, tunnels, and walls for the ball to go over, through, or around on its way to the hole. Use your own ideas!

Rules

The rules for backyard golf are simple. Begin at the starting spot (tee) for the first hole. Use your club to hit the ball and make it roll into the hole. (It will usually take more than one hit.) Count the number of times you hit the ball. The fewer times you hit it, the better you are. In this game, the low score wins! Have fun, and remember—keep calm, like Uncle Scrooge.

Riding the Duckburg Express

"Can't catch me," yelled Louie as he zipped downstairs past Uncle Scrooge.

Zip! Zip! Huey and Dewey went running after him.

"You boys need to let off a little steam," Uncle Scrooge said. "Steam—that reminds me of the old steam engines and the great trains we had when I was a boy. That's it! We'll make a train in the backyard."

They did—and it didn't cost Uncle Scrooge a cent.

An Old-Fashioned Steam Engine

What you'll need

2 cardboard cartons (medium size)	Tape
Salt box	Black paint
	Scissors or knife

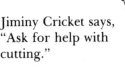

Jiminy Cricket says, "Ask for help with cutting."

1. Cut the two short flaps off of one box. Lean the two long flaps toward each other and tape the short flaps between them, as shown.

2. Set the second box up on end against the end of the first box. Open the flaps and tape them together.

3. Tape the boxes together. Then tape the salt box to the top of the first box.

4. Paint the boxes black, and you have a steam engine!

Passenger cars. Just line up some straight-backed chairs in a row behind the engine. To make your train special, put a seat cover on each chair. Make the cover by cutting two pieces the same size from large grocery bags. Tape them together on three sides. Decorate each seat cover with the name of your railroad. Slip the cover over the back of a chair.

Special touches. Make tickets from scraps of paper. Print the words *Conductor* and *Engineer* on pieces of cardboard and fasten them to old hats or baseball caps. Now your train is ready to roll. All aboard!

Windplay

There are two things Uncle Scrooge doesn't like about shopping. First, he has to spend money. Second, the dollar bills he gets in change are often dirty.

One day after shopping, Uncle Scrooge sat in the backyard watching his freshly washed dollar bills on the clothesline dance gently in the wind. After the difficult task of washing all that money, he was looking for something relaxing to do. The bills bouncing in the breeze gave him an idea. He'd make other things that would float in the wind! Here are some things Uncle Scrooge did. Why not try them yourself?

Soap Bubbles

Fill a small jar three-quarters full with water. Add a few squirts of liquid detergent and a drop of cooking oil and stir. Dip a straw in the water. Now take it out and blow through the end that isn't wet. Watch the wind take the bubbles and bounce them gently across the yard. When you have finished, cover the jar and save the bubble mixture for another time.

Paper Airplane

What you'll need

Typing paper
Crayons

1. Fold a sheet of typing paper in half lengthwise.

2. Fold the two corners on the same end up to the center fold.

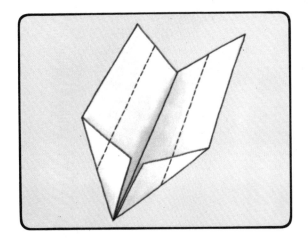

3. Fold each side down to the bottom edge.

4. Color your plane.

5. Spread the wings. Throw the plane by holding it underneath and smoothly flinging it forward.

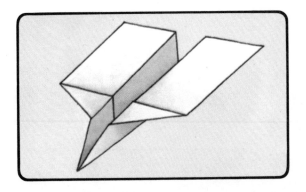

Snow Business

On a snowy winter evening, Donald Duck came over to help Uncle Scrooge plan Duckburg's Winter Carnival. As Donald walked in, he stomped the snow off his feet, rubbed his hands together, and said, "C-C-Cold outside."

When Uncle Scrooge heard that, he yelled, "Gold outside!" and dived straight out the front door.

Ten minutes later, Uncle Scrooge was back in, covered with so much snow that he looked like a snowman—or a snow duck. "Donald," he said, "there's no gold outside."

"That wasn't what I said, Uncle Scrooge," Donald laughed. "But you certainly look like the gold medal winner in the Winter Carnival snow statue contest!"

Backyard fun isn't just for warm weather. If you're looking for cold-weather fun, plan a winter carnival. Tell your friends to bundle up and come over for some snow games. Or use just one or two of these ideas to warm up a winter afternoon.

Take a strong, small box and pack it tightly with snow. Now quickly turn the box upside down on the ground and carefully lift it up. What's left is a snow block.

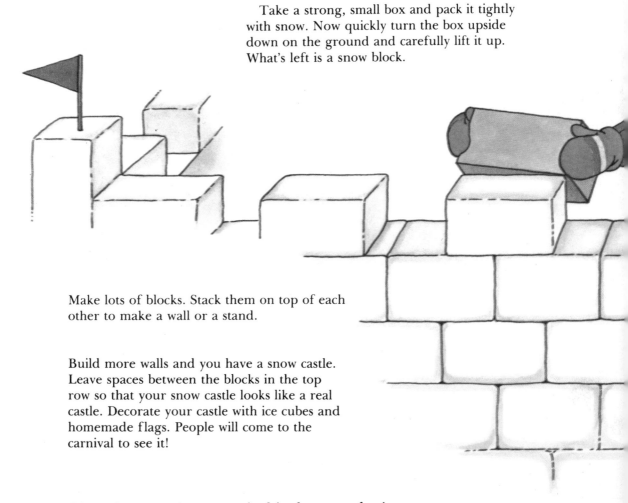

Make lots of blocks. Stack them on top of each other to make a wall or a stand.

Build more walls and you have a snow castle. Leave spaces between the blocks in the top row so that your snow castle looks like a real castle. Decorate your castle with ice cubes and homemade flags. People will come to the carnival to see it!

One nice thing about a winter carnival is that you don't need to bring tables outside. You can make stands and booths out of snow blocks.

If you have games, make some prizes to give to winners. You can make medals like the ones on page 29 and decorate them with winter carnival pictures. Here are some contest ideas.

Snowman-Building Contest

Have your neighborhood friends make snowmen in their own yards. Have other friends walk around and judge the snowmen. The judges can give awards for the Best-Looking Snowman, the Funniest-Looking Snowman, the Biggest Snowman, and the Most Unusual Snowman.

Snowball-Throwing Contest

Make a chest-high stand out of snow bricks. On top of the stand set brightly colored plastic bottles. Several feet away from the stand, build a low, narrow fence of snow blocks. Each player makes three snowballs and throws from behind the fence to try to knock down the bottles.

Two-Person Sled Race

This is a team race. One person rides on the sled and a second person pushes it. Make a course on flat ground, and use a brightly colored ribbon for the finish line.

You can brighten up your winter carnival by decorating with colorful flags and streamers. And you can warm it up by serving hot cider or chocolate. A winter carnival parade would be fun, too. Instead of decorating bikes, decorate sleds and toboggans. Have fun and keep warm!